The Candlestick Wars

Tim Buchanan

COMMUNICATE
FORWARD

To Pamela. The line where you end and I begin has long since disappeared and we have become one in a way I never could have imagined. You have always been my magic. I love you.

Get ready!

The War Begins

Once upon a time in a land called Opportunity, there lived a butcher, a baker, and TWO candlestick makers. Yes, two candlestick makers. The butcher and the baker were living happily ever after because they each had a monopoly.

However, the candlestick makers were unhappy because there was not enough business for both of them. One would be the loser; the other would be the winner. Or maybe both would be losers. And so the war began.

How uncivilized is that? Isn't there enough business to go around for everyone? Isn't it possible to work together and make the world peachy for everyone to do business in? I don't think so. The reality is, you can't avoid competition. You can't even park your car without someone else wanting to take a closer parking space. You compete for time, money, a promotion, goods, services, customers, donors, attention, space, and even a spouse. Competition is just a nice name for a war. So let's just call it a war and be done with it.

"Hey," you ask, "what's with all the 'once-upon-a-time' stuff and war?" You probably just want the hard facts about business and not a story. But facts are just useless pieces of information until you have a proper framework to hang them on. Our framework is going to be the war between these two candlestick makers because you will recognize the battles of your competitive war only through their story. Actually, if you don't first learn how to fight the war of competition in your own land, then thinking you'll have a successful business is the real fairy tale.

But let's get back to the two candlestick makers. They were fairly evenly matched. They both had plenty of experience in the trade, and both made a decent product. *Hmm ...* now you're thinking this will be a boring story. Actually, most businesses are boring, and they trudge along in mediocrity. Few of them know how to break from the pack and begin to really win big. So, that is what I am going to build my story around. I am going to show you how one of these merchants was able to win big. Isn't that what you want to do in your business? You never started your business or career with the goal of being mediocre. You didn't want to simply win a consolation prize. You wanted success, and you still do. You want to know how to become successful. So let's see what the candlestick makers did.

But first, let's give these two merchants a name. I feel a PC crisis coming on. Do I make them women, men, young, old, or what? Well, let's call one Anne and the other Bill. Now I have to figure out who wins and who loses. I know, I'll flip a coin. Done!

Also, we have to level the playing field and eliminate all the other competitive issues. We don't have enough space in this book to discuss all the details of an epic war. Let's just say Anne and Bill have the same experience, supply chain, material and labor costs. We are going to limit the scope of this war to one issue, how well they communicate in the marketplace. Companies will spend millions gaining in these other areas, and that is good. But, if you cannot communicate in the marketplace, you must have a huge differential factor in some other area. Most businesses don't have that.

Think about it a minute, how important is communication in warfare? If the lines of communication are cut, then all coordination, provision, and strategy come to a screeching halt. Is there anything in your business that doesn't depend on communication? A scientist convinced the business world years ago that communication was a "soft" skill. That's a lie. It is one of the strongest and hardest skills you can ever develop internally or externally in your business. You may forget a hundred times that this book is about communication. Determine that you will not do so! You have to remember that your effectiveness in any marketplace is totally dependent on your conversation with the market, both verbal and nonverbal.

Oh, I almost forgot, you need to know who won the coin toss. Read on and you will see ...

Make a Difference

to be known

Bill and Anne are in a new market, and they need to get known by the consumers - quickly. They both know that first impressions are lasting impressions. They also know they have to be differentiated in the marketplace and for every day that they aren't, it's going to cost them a lot of money. This is not the only hurdle they face, but it's a big and ongoing challenge. As is the case in every business, Bill and Anne's identities will be on the line every day.

Candlestick makers are the engineers of times past. Even though they are simple merchants, they still have to follow processes. They experience design and production issues, and just as you are wrapped up in the "science" of your job or business, Bill and Anne must learn their market quickly so they can move on to the real work of running a business and making a profit. This is precisely where many companies die before they have fully taken their first breath.

Getting known in the marketplace is critical for any business. You probably classify this as branding. Most businesses, well the smart ones anyway, put a lot of time, effort, and money into this process. This is where most businesses go wrong. The first and biggest mistake they make is viewing the task of branding as a mechanical/scientific/hard skill event.

Corporations and small businesses pick a name and a tag line by an analytical process. They might use focus groups (which often are not truthful), surveys, or brilliant advertising minds. Now, if this really worked, businesses that use this approach would not fail—and yet many do.

Their approach is all wrong. Getting known in your market is not a mechanical or scientific event. Brochures and advertising alone do not guarantee success. As important as they may be, market awareness does not come from a single process or a one-time event. A business should not launch itself, but instead introduce itself. Instead of declaring yourself, you need to explain yourself. Finding your niche in the marketplace is not a matter of establishing a beachhead but simply arranging your first date. It is not so much about staking a claim as it is about asking the consumers to dance. We fail when we perceive business as a transaction instead of a relationship in today's marketplace. Successful marketing starts with the tone you set about yourself.

Bill's Introduction to the Market

Bill lost the coin toss. Now he is going to do everything, well, most everything, wrong. I knew you would figure this all out later, but I couldn't wait to tell you. I'm terrible at keeping secrets. You might wonder why I would relate his story. After all, no one likes to read about a loser. But as you read, you have to remember that Bill's story and the way he does things is just as important as Anne's; because you need to learn from him, too. I want you to think of Bill's marketing efforts as the rumble bars on the side of the roadway. You are smarter in business if you know you are approaching danger before you actually are in danger. Besides, more people can identify with the way Bill does things because many people are not communicating well in the marketplace.

We can learn a lot by the way someone introduces himself. If someone introduces himself to me and uses words like "just" to describe their job or "little" to describe their business, I reprimand them! They need to take a higher view of what they do. Recently, one of my graduate students was one of three final interviewees for a promotion. In our conversation, he said, "The strongest candidate for this job is a guy from Stanford (not the college where I teach) and ..." I stopped him, and asked, "Who is the strongest candidate?" He replied, "A guy from Stanford." I said, "I am going to ask this only one more time ..." "Oh," he said, "I am the strongest candidate." "And if you don't believe that," I said, "then you need to drop out now because you will interview like someone who doesn't believe they should have the job."

You can also tell a lot about a company, organization, or person by the way they describe themselves. Let's see how Bill describes his new business.

Bill's Candle Shoppe

Serving You With Over 20 Years of Candle Making Experience

While you might not rank this as the greatest sign in the world, you might not think it's all that bad either. I mean, to the average businessperson, the sign conveys service and experience. What could be wrong with that? Many businesses have a long and distinguished history they are proud of. Bill is letting people know he has the expertise to back up his business. He is trying to tell them how good he is and that they would be wise to use his services for all their candle needs. The only problem is, his sign speaks volumes to him and little to the marketplace.

Some vehemently disagree with my conclusion, so let's consider a recent case study. All politics aside, let's look at the 2008 presidential campaign. Hands down, McCain's history and experience dwarfed Obama's. When I asked a classroom of liberal Obama supporting MBA students if they were the hiring committee for the office of President, would they have taken even a second look at Obama based on his history and experience, they answered with a resounding "No". Now, if past history and experience is so overwhelmingly important, why isn't John McCain in the White House today? Because history and experience do not matter to most people.

People don't care what kind of car their dad drove or where he bought it. They don't have a family butcher, department store, or church. If you look at the parents of adult children today, they have at least two cars and probably not the same brand. They also have multiple TVs, and again, not the same brand. It is naive for a company to think long-term brand loyalty exists today.

Think about it, you are probably just like me. I own three different brands of TVs. I have a foreign and a domestic car. I have a Windows computer and a Mac computer. The harsh reality is, people don't care how long you have been doing anything today; so deal with it, and move on!

Does My Experience Have Any Value?

So now you wonder if your experience matters at all. It seems from what I have said that anyone can enter the marketplace and blow you away with little or no experience. But that's not what I said. Don't get ahead of me. Your history and experience play a very big role in marketing just as it does for Bill's Candles. What I said was that it does not matter to the marketplace as a selling point. It is not a strong lure to snag today's consumers. You are going to waste valuable marketing space and money if you keep telling people what you have done in the past.

Look at this phenomenon in a different light. Remember how I said this was a relationship you are trying to build and not just a transaction you are trying to have? Think about it in those terms. What do you think would happen if a young man, let's call him Jim, wanted to ask a pretty girl out that he had seen at the gym? He decides he is going to make his move and ask her out. He times his move just right, and catches the girl coming out of the gym. "Hi", he says, "my name is Jim, and I have been a man for 27 years". "Hello", she answers back, looking around to see if there is someone else close by. Jim continues, "I would like to ask you out for dinner. I have been dating women for more than ten years and have been buying meals at restaurants for nearly as long. I will pick you up in my car that I have owned for three years. If you like, I will be glad to show you the maintenance records before you enter the automobile". Need I say more about the lunacy of Jim's approach? But does this kind of approach make any more sense for a company?

Just because your history and experience are not initial marketing tools doesn't mean they aren't valuable. Often, you will find people telling others what they most want or need to hear themselves. When we are in competitive situations, we often experience some self-doubt and fear. Like my student who was bucking for a promotion, sometimes we lack the confidence we need. We don't want to appear cocky, but we have to appear confident or others will see our self-doubt and avoid us. Often, individuals and companies extol their history and/or experience because of their internal need for reassurance. It's like they're saying out loud, "I think I can, I think I can." It is not the way to reach the marketplace.

All these things are valuable in two other arenas. You do, indeed, need to know what you are capable of doing. You, your leaders, and your employees need to have a clear and confident image of your core competencies and how they were developed. This is where the internal confidence comes into play. Talk about these things in-house, and don't be afraid to tell stories of past victories and accomplishments. Sing your praises inside but not in the marketplace. The consumers were not there in the past. They don't care what happened back then. They are concerned about tomorrow. When and if Bill gets a big candle order, he needs to know he can fulfill it in a timely and quality manner. He can't go out and get business he is unsure about servicing.

You also have to remember that you will have your time and place to tell your customers more about your past. As the relationship grows, the conversation will evolve into something more in-depth. Depending on the amount of money someone is spending with you, the conversation will go into depth proportionally. If someone is buying a T-shirt from you, he is not going to get very intimate. If someone is spending 200 million dollars with you, he is going to find out a lot about you. Remember, though, if you approach business as a growing relationship rather than a simple transaction, you will let it evolve in a relationship framework and timeline.

Anne's Introduction to the Market

> # Anne's Candle Shoppe
> ### Bringing Elegant Lighting Into Your Home

At first glance, there doesn't seem to be much difference in Anne's sign and Bill's, but a closer look reveals a lot of difference. Bill talked about what he was capable of doing, Anne talked about what it would mean for the customers. Bill talked about doing something. Anne talked about changing something. One message was self-centered, the other was focused on the customers. The first expected the consumers to connect the product to themselves; the latter did it for them. This huge difference in the approach of the two candlestick makers explains the huge difference in the two signs. Bill focused on what he could do, whereas Anne focused on the impact she could have. Similarly, there's a huge difference between claiming to produce a great widget and claiming to greatly improve people's lives. So, to be successful, companies and organizations must make a seismic paradigm shift!

When was the last time you thought seriously about the difference you're making in the world? You may spend a lot of time on supply chain management, marketing, customer acquisition, market share, environmental compliance, research, and development, but how much time do you devote to thinking about the positive impact you are making in your customer's life? You are missing a big opportunity if you aren't thinking about this impact, because your customers, or potential customers, *are* thinking about it. In fact, the impact you make in their life is about the only thing they think about, and it is precisely how they identify you. When was the last time you bought a product from someone just because they had great supply chain management? Probably never!

If you think you are on top of your relationship with your customers because you have Customer Relationship Management (CRM) software, you need to think again. What I am talking about goes way beyond this technology because it is interpersonal. CRM manages the mechanics and transactions of your relationship to your customers, but it does not define or create the relationship. CRM software can measure and track your impact with customers, but cannot substitute for the core company identity based on making a difference in others' lives. Most companies have a better relationship with their

CRM software than they do with their actual customers. They know more about the demographics of their customers than they do about their customers' real needs. Impact is more than just trying to track if someone is coming back on a predetermined interval for another order.

Yes, those things are important, and they do determine the impact you can make in your customer's life. If Walmart®[1] did not have a strong supply chain, CRM, and distribution management system, it could not overpower the market as it does. But, its management practices are not the reason people shop at Walmart. They shop there because they can have a little bigger piece of the American Dream on their limited income. They can acquire more things that bring them pleasure. So, every time you consider doing something new at your company, you have to ask yourself how it will impact your customers. That question is what should be setting your company's direction and strategies.

Is Vision Enough?

Your company probably has a vision or mission statement, but have you read it recently? How many of your employees know what it says? Vision/mission statements have become the biggest fad with the least amount of bang. Those who originally proposed them had something much different in mind than how businesses use them. I believe the original intent was sound and practical and could have made a great difference if the concept had been understood and used correctly. I'm afraid the problem concerns the name of the tool and not the instrument itself. The term "vision" or "mission" made it seem futuristic and metaphysical. People just could not connect it to the here and now.

Today, business happens so quickly that you need to have your head in the present as well as the future. Now we have to focus on business foresight rather than vision. It is much harder today to predict where things will go, and more importantly to be more adaptable and nimble than prophetic. The rapid changes in technology mean that it is harder to leap very far into the future with a new product. Shortened product-life cycles and the sheer speed of obsolescence translate to rapid business outcomes of either upward mobility or downward mortality.

Markets and economies have become globally self-aware. No one really owns or controls them any longer. Now, businesses simply have a relationship with the market instead of control of it. Consumers expect business to manage the new technologies and be as nimble as possible through your relationship management with said markets. They are not only constantly assessing your relationship to the market, but also to them, the consumers. The implication is huge: businesses have to start seeing themselves as a conduit between the consumer and the market. This conduit is a relationship, and your effectiveness in managing these relationships is the measure of your impact in others' lives. Impact is your identity.

What's Bill going to do when candles become obsolete? He has identified himself as an experienced candle maker. Anne has identified herself as someone who impacts the everyday life of her customers with elegant lighting. Bill is selling candles and Anne is providing home lighting. Think about your business for a minute. Are you selling something of limited scope while hoping for a successful future? Are you providing something with a long-term impact? Employees don't know what your vision is for tomorrow, and your customers don't care. They only want to know what impact you are going to make in their lives today and whether it is sustainable.

Nike®[2] does not sell tennis shoes or sports apparel. It provides the tools necessary to be a winner! The sports apparel business and raw materials can change, but Nike will still be making an impact. One day, when our great-great-grandchildren are wearing anti-gravity footwear and shooting at goals fifty feet off the ground, Nike will still be making an impact by providing the tools to be a winner. What is your impact, and how much have you limited yourself?

Relationship and Impact Stealers

I once heard about a woman who went on a date with a body builder. The night was a great disappointment because she spent the whole evening watching him admire himself in every reflective surface they passed. He ignored her completely because he loved himself so much. Businesses do the same thing when they become more focused on internal processes than they are on their relationships in the marketplace. Internal processes are important, but not if it causes you to ignore your customers.

If you are solely focused on your processes, your identity and connection with customers will suffer. If you are totally committed to the impact you make in your customer's lives, then you will create the processes to sustain your impact. It is not a matter of ignoring your processes, but of giving them a reason to thrive. Processes should support your impact, not supersede it.

Microsoft®[3] has been driven by an operating system since its inception. You could argue that even though the product has its critics, Microsoft's focus has been very profitable. Well, so far it has. Soon, though, people will want to do a lot more cloud computing and not be tied to a single machine in a single locale. Mobile computing is here to stay.

The marketplace is changing and Microsoft still seems to be focused on operating systems. Some predict that this may lead to its downfall. No one should be so naive as to predict Microsoft could not be eclipsed. That is just the world we live in today. Microsoft could suffer if it has the same mindset as Bill the candle maker. (Hey, I just made the connection too.) Microsoft appears to be product driven, not impact driven.

Without inferring any preference (I use and own both products), consider Apple®[4]. They started in a head to head platform war with Microsoft. Yet in recent years, they have shifted from an operating system focus to a host of blockbuster products. Apple seems to have freed itself from a single product line and focused on impact. While Microsoft is associated with an operating system, Apple is associated with cutting edge innovations.

You have to make the decision that it is better to have a strong identity and relationship in the marketplace than it is to have a strong tie to a product or profit margin. A product driven company can do very well for a while, but it is not sustainable. It has a smash-and-grab mentality. Smash the market, grab all the profits you can, and then disappear. Is that the impact you want to make?

Beyond Rebranding

Many companies think they need to rebrand. Maybe they do, but most companies need a new identity rather than a new brand. What's the difference? Rebranding is like getting a new suit because the old one no longer fits. The problem isn't the old suit, but you needing to lose a few pounds. Many companies want to change the way they are perceived in the marketplace, when they really need to change how they function. You have to do more than just put a coat of fresh paint on the tired old frame. You have to change your identity.

Do you think people in your company right now can tell you the impact they make in others' lives and what part they personally play in that impact? What if you were a soft drink company and they thought their only job was to sell sodas and make a profit for the shareholders?

Twenty-five years ago I worked with high-school kids. We were going to have a summer outing at the lake and I saw an attention-getting soft drink ad. It showed two inner tubes tied together with people rolling down a hill inside them and dropping into a lake. I thought, why not? So I got a couple of inner tubes, tied them together, and took them along. We found a great hill and the first sucker, err, kid climbed in. Some of us pushed and rolled him down the hill and into the lake. Aside from the fact that we could have killed someone, we laughed until we cried. If only we had video cameras and AFV back then. I will never forget that incident, nor will those kids, some of whom are still my friends. Also, I will never forget the name of the soda featured in the ad. I will forever associate it with fun and carefree living. The soda company made an impact beyond brand recognition because it ran a whole series of ads about fun things to do with friends. If I still drank soda, I would drink theirs.

You see, everything you do as a company, and every department and person in your company has the potential to make an impact in others' lives. What customers are you missing if you don't see that? Anyone can make a candlestick, but how many will light your home with elegance? Anyone can do what your company does, so what's to keep people from patronizing them instead of you? The only thing is, they have to see you will make a bigger impact in their life with your product than the next company will with its product.

Bill and Anne's businesses sit right next to each other, and they both make and sell candles. Bill offers a product, and Anne offers to make a difference in her customers' homes. Bill wants to _sell_ something. Anne wants to _do_ something. Bill is saying let me provide you with something you need. Anne is saying let me help you with something that is important to you. Anne goes beyond branding—s*he really cares and wants to help people.*

What difference are you making in people's lives? What is your impact in this world as a person, a company, or an organization? That is how you will be identified, known, and remembered. The great thing is that it is up to you to decide what difference you are going to make with the product, service, or idea that you have. If you start everything with, "How much money can I make?" you will make some money but not much. What if you start your product development, meetings, or day with, "What impact can we make?"

Instead of a new coat of paint on top of all the other coats you've applied over the years, why not do some real remodeling of your company? Try rebuilding the paradigms that have held you back all these years. Start identifying yourself by the difference you make every time you sign a contract or deliver a product. Instead of people coming to work for a paycheck, help them come to work with the purpose of making someone's life a little better because they did their job today. They won't do it until the leaders do, so show them the way.

What impact can you really make in your marketplace? That is exactly who you are and how everyone else knows you. What would happen if everyone in your company knew this?

Share Passion

to be attractive

Bill thought Anne's sign was kind of silly. Even though Anne had just as much experience as Bill, he felt she was foolish to not place her credentials on the sign. In his mind, it was just another indicator of how fast he would reach his goals. You see, this was the first candle company Bill had owned. He had worked his whole life for a big candle maker in the city. Not only had he made the candles, but he was also the bookkeeper for the company.

Bill knew firsthand how to make a quality candle efficiently and how much profit was in it. All he could think about for years was getting his chance to make a quality product and earn a fair profit for his family and himself. He had long since worked out the details of how he would manufacture and market his candles. So this is where his passion lay.

To discover a person's passion, just figure out what consumes most of his thoughts. It is something he daydreams about, lies awake at night thinking about, and wakes up in the morning with it on his mind. Our passions consume us and all our thoughts. Bill couldn't wait for the chance to put all his ideas into motion. He had designed his candle shop a million times in his head. Once he actually had a shop, it took him no time at all to lay it all out and get production going. He would have an efficient and productive shop. He made sure that his entire shop was visible from the front windows of the store. He wanted everyone to walk by and see his great candle-making process. People would appreciate his state-of-the-art shop and techniques. When people stopped by the shop, Bill would tell them all the things he knew about making a good candle. He would tell them they would be wise to buy from him.

Bill was in love with his business. His passion was all about making candles. But no matter how carefully he explained his process to people, business was slow. Every night, Bill compiled a list of all the benefits his candles had over Anne's. The next day, he would recite the list to potential customers. He never mentioned Anne or her shop; he just made sure everyone knew what made his candles better. Bill was consumed with making his candles, and he could not wait to reap the profit from them.

What's Wrong with Quality?

I like a quality product as much as the next person. If people didn't appreciate quality, all the consumer websites would be out of business. But the importance of quality comes much later in the customer relationship and not right at the start. It is very important, but not so much now. Bill has made a classic mistake. He talks about his perceived benefits, but no one is interested in those.

It's like our young man who was trying to get a date. He could take a girl to the finest restaurant in town and provide a very high quality meal along with a ride in a limo and the best flowers money could buy. While she might enjoy herself, if there is no chemistry between them, she is not going out with him again. On the other hand, I have been married more than 30 years, and my wife really likes a nice night out on the town. So, what is the difference? Timing.

Your internal passion is not enough to drive the consumer. In the 1980s, Ford®[5] coined the slogan, *Quality is Job1*[6]. This was a rebranding effort around their shift to Total Quality Management. To me, using this as a slogan begs to ask why they had to remind themselves and us of this. I mean, do you want to hurl your family down the interstate at 70 miles per hour in a car they have to remind themselves to put together right? They did need to improve this aspect of their business because, as I said, quality is important. Their sales increased when they returned their product to a competitive level of dependability. Ford made great strides in this area, and then a downturn in the economy severely hurt the big three American automakers. What happened to Ford? Did people quit caring about quality? No. So why did their sales drop? Because they had only met the expectations of the marketplace (a safe and quality car, but many similar safe, well-built cars were available). But when the economy tanked in 2009, Ford had to drop their slogan because it was not enough to really sell cars.

The test of any company comes when things are tough. This is the test Bill is in right now with his fledgling candle company. Ford had to change emphasis and get a relationship going with the customers, just as Bill needs to. He has to offer something more than what people basically expect. There are way too many choices in the marketplace today for those who don't offer a quality product to survive. With the way the Internet has supercharged the law of the invisible hand, poor quality will cause you to be history in no time flat.

Years ago, quality was a deciding issue, because quality was not always guaranteed in the early days of the industrial or technology revolutions. It's no longer a real differentiator, but an expected part of every product.

Even so, Bill would point out to people how his wax was kept at just the right temperature and how he precisely timed the intervals between candle dippings to insure the greatest wax buildup each time. People would politely listen to Bill and then roll their eyes when they finally left the shop. Are you boring your customers with details about quality?

If all your passion is inside the business, you aren't going to appeal to your customers. You can market all you want, but you and the consumers have nothing in common except the money you hope to get from them. It sounds crude, but that is all many companies and organizations care about. Hey, you have to live with yourself, not me. If we have to be in business and make a profit, which is great, can't we care about something other than ourselves? Unfortunately, one weakness of a free market is corporate narcissism. Which would you rather buy from: a company that is selling you something only to make a profit or a company that is providing you with something you care about while it makes a profit?

Bill cared about what was important to Bill and expected others to share his passion. That's not going to fly in today's marketplace, so you might have to go through a twelve-step program to break the company of its narcissism. I'll be looking for that support group phone number, but in the meantime, what in the world is Anne doing?

Is Sharing So Bad?

Before you paint me a warm-fuzzy-let's-all-hold-hands-and-sing-together-softy guy, there is something you should know about me. I am a fierce competitor in all things. I will draw blood over Ping-Pong. I don't believe in good losers, just people who are good at losing. I don't think you should shout, "That's okay. You'll get the next one" to the little kid in the outfield who has laid down his glove to pick clover while he is oblivious to the ball rolling by him and the runners are rounding the bases. Get that kid a musical instrument or an art set to find his real talent, but for heaven's sake get him off the ball field. He isn't an athlete! Whew, I have wanted to say that for a very long time.

Anne is not a softy; she is just plain smart. She knows that people expect her to make a quality candle. She knows she has to be efficient in her manufacturing process or she will not be able to maintain her margins. She knows she has to make a fair profit to stay in business. She also knows she is the one who cares about that, but her customers don't. Finally, she knows she will fail if she doesn't connect on some level of passion with her customers. She has to find where her interest and the consumers' interest intersect in order to capitalize on it.

Anne knew exactly where she wanted to meet her audience. She decided to use her window space to show how well a home or shop could be lighted with the right candles in the right place. She arranged part of her window like a parlor and the other half like a shop so she could appeal to both the men and the women in town. She lit areas with as few candles as possible. She changed the settings from time to time. Sometimes she would show a clerk's office, and at other times a kitchen. She wanted people to see how much better their home could be lit for work and pleasure.

Bill walked by her windows one day and kind of snorted as he shook his head. This was the silliest thing he had ever seen. Why would anyone buy from Anne without seeing her shop? How did she expect to sell a good product when she wasted all her time on these foolish little settings? He had a good idea whose shop would be the last one standing, and it wasn't going to be Anne's. He was glad he had a good business head and paid attention to the details of actually making his candles.

Other people would stop by Anne's shop also. Many of them would point out things they liked. Men and women would mill around the window because they wanted their homes well lit like the scenes in Anne's shop window. Often, they would step in and ask her questions. Anne would always stop and talk about how and why she had positioned the candles in the display. She would ask the customers about their homes and needs. People liked to stay in Anne's shop and talk because they had a shared interest.

This is the secret of great business. Your passion has go beyond finding your spot to also finding exactly what your customers need. Anne already wanted to impact an area of her customers' lives, and that desire led right to their passion. Her passion was making sure that people's homes were well lit. She did not just want them to buy her candles, but to meet a need.

On the other hand, Bill thought meeting customers' needs was kind of implied and silly for him to exploit. Wait, did I just insinuate exploitation of Anne's customers? No, I simply stated that she was exploiting the opportunity where she and her customers shared a passion. That's just plain smart in my book.

The point where you can identify your audience's shared passion is the sweet spot of business, because they are bringing a perception of added value to the table.

You can't let that opportunity go by. You will look for it if you are really smart and ambitious. You can't fake your passion for it because the marketplace will never forgive you for deceiving them. But if you are truly sincere, find it. This is exactly what happens when someone successfully mines a niche market. They find a passion they share with a small group of people and converge on that point as merchant and customer.

Remember the 2008 presidential campaign? McCain talked on and on about his history and experience and what "he" wanted to do with America. Obama just smiled and wanted to make a change and America shared his passion for what must change. Once again, think who won. He was not the first less-qualified candidate to use this same method of impact and shared passion to win. Kennedy and Reagan did the same thing and won against opponents who had more experience. They found the sweet spot of intersection and capitalized on it big time.

All the other things in your business are still important, but not as important as where your passion meets the marketplace. If you don't care about those other things, you won't be able to meet people at the intersection anymore. So keep paying attention to the details, but start looking for that place where you can build a common passion with your customers. This is where the real success begins. This is the easiest portal you will ever find to send your products and services through. You have to care enough to take the time to find this place.

Start by finding ways to demonstrate your passion. Just like Anne's front store window, have a place where people can walk by and see what you are doing. Like her, you might have to use some trial and error to find just the right things that peak their interest. You will have to spend time listening to them and find out what they are looking for. At first, you might not hit on it, but keep trying until you find it. Listen and watch until you see the shared point that is most important to them.

If you still don't believe me, try using your whole advertising budget for the next month talking about your supply chain management or accounting software and see how your business explodes. We both know that's silly, so start looking for a better place. Tell me, which would you think is easier: to convince the marketplace that they need your product or to find a way your product meets a need they already have? Just bring them into the conversation, and they will think up more ways to use your product than you can. Tap into their passion and need, and they will tap into your product or service.

What if your company could lay a foundation that will serve you well in any market or endeavor. What would change if your employees could understand what your impact is and where your passion meets with the marketplace? Don't be a Bill, get out there and make something happen the smart way and soon your people will be working on a whole new level with your customers.

Customers. I almost forgot them. We have been doing "things" to promote the business and attract the people but we haven't discussed them in much detail. Hmm, do we have to? I mean, people can be so much trouble. Do we really have to get to know them that well? Do we have to talk to them and let them in on this whole thing? They are such a messy detail of business. Most like it better when people are just a sales number or a demographic. Well, we could reduce them to a number, but that would not only make this a short book, but also one without the whole story of success. Remember, this is all about a relationship and not a transaction, so we have to talk about people. Brace yourself and turn the page.

Value Others

to show sincerity

In this war, you must win two deciding battles. The first is against yourself and all your tendencies to get in your own way. Later, we will identify and discuss the second one. To be really successful, you have to get beyond the internal things that hold you back. Bill and Anne have to win the battles in themselves if they want to win the war for success. You never can actually beat your competition, you just win the war in yourself and your company before they do and move ahead. That's all. When you win the war in you, you and your customers will share the spoils of war.

Bill is making decisions against himself and he is unaware of it. Like so many, he has gone into business exclusively for himself. He saw a market to be penetrated and conquered. Don't be like Bill. You can be all business if you want, but ultimately, you have to be concerned about someone else. People who invest their lives in business to the exclusion of all else are never winners. Business people who think there is nothing in this world besides their company are really big losers. You cannot build a great company without caring about others. You may build a big one, but never a great one, because the attitude of the company is passed right through the employees to the customers who ultimately decide your greatness.

Until the time Anne and Bill opened their shops, people in the Land of Opportunity bought all of their candles from a traveling salesman who came around once a month with his wagon full of wares. His candles were a very common kind that all looked the same. Each one was long, slender, and white. Sometimes, if the salesman's inventory was low, the candles were old and somewhat bent from getting hot and bounced around in the wagon. Sometimes, they stuck together. The people of the town did not like these poor quality candles, but it was their only choice before Bill and Anne's shops opened. Suddenly, they had another choice.

Bill's Approach to Others

If business really is a complex relationship, rather than a simple transaction, Bill's attitude towards others is paramount to his success. His primary question when considering his market is:

"How much of my product can or will they buy"? Now, obviously he cannot sell candles made for kings to the common class. He must have a product in the price range his market can afford. However, the issue of Bill's perceived value of the customer to his business is most critical because it will drive his actions. Get that! *His perception of other's perceived value will drive his actions.*

Have you ever had to be around someone you really did not like? Perhaps you told yourself that you were a professional and you could be cordial and no one would know your true feelings. I'll bet you told yourself that until you believed it, didn't you? The joke's on you, because no matter how hard you tried, those inner perceptions drove your every move, gesture, and nonverbal cue. Next time, just be honest with yourself and decide to be as polite as possible without the delusion of thinking you are hiding your true feelings.

Bill fundamentally thought that people had to be stupid to keep buying from the traveling salesman. He had posted a flyer in his shop showing the value of the salesman's cheap candles and that of his own quality candles. He would show it to every person who came into the shop and explain in great detail the price per hour of burning one of his candles compared to the cheap ones. In fact, he had even placed one of the bent and discolored candles next to one of his finest candles. Above this display, he placed a sign: "Which would you rather have in your home?" Bill assumed that anyone who really cared about his family and his money would naturally buy from Bill's Candle Shoppe.

When Bill saw people on the street, he would sometimes ask them if they were still wasting their money on the cheap candles from the "tin man." He was growing increasingly frustrated with the town's people. In his mind, it became a battle against them and their stupidity. He knew they needed to be presented with benefits and he could think of no greater benefit than the cost savings of a better candle. He thought these people were kind of dumb. Since he had started this whole venture with a seed of cynicism, it was easy for things to make it grow. His demeanor towards the marketplace became more adversarial with every passing day.

This is how it happens. If you don't realize the battles that wage war in your own mind, you will begin to see the war between you and others instead of with yourself.

It was clear to all the town's people that they were simply a prospective sale for Bill. They would avoid him every chance they got because he would pounce on them about their candles. Bill actually thought he was being a good salesman and representative for his product. I mean, if you don't believe in something, you can't sell it. But Bill didn't value the people in the town. He thought they were something to be conquered instead of people to be brought into a relationship. They were a means of keeping score for him and not individuals he could share his talents with. These people had a need that he could fill if they would just part with their money. He would value them only if they became his customers and not a minute sooner. Bill respected only those who recognized his worth and the worth of his candles.

As far as Bill was concerned, there was only one right choice these people could make, and that was to buy from Bill's Candle Shoppe. I mean, really, what did these commoners know about candles anyway? If they would just come into Bill's shop, he would get them the right candles for their homes and send them on their merry way. Didn't they understand that he was just trying to help them? It wasn't like he was trying to cheat them or anything. In fact, in Bill's mind, the traveling salesman was the one who was cheating them by selling pathetic old candles that burned up almost as fast as you could light them.

Occasionally, Bill would make a few sales. Sometimes people bought a few candles just to get out of his shop. Others were actually value conscious and saw the logic of using a better candle. After all, Bill was indeed a very fine candlestick maker. He would always remind them, as he filled out the sales slip, to be sure and let everyone know where they got their candles. He would tell them once or twice more before they got out of the store. Sometimes he would even call after them as they walked away.

Bill was proud of his candles, and he wanted everyone to know they came from his shop. Besides, everyone knows how important word of mouth advertising is, so Bill just wanted to prod it along.

Anne's Approach to Others

I'll bet you already figured out that, unlike Bill, Anne is going to do everything right. You are just too smart for me, aren't you? But rather than depart from Bill too quickly and write him off as the bad guy, I want you to reflect on him just a little. The fact is there is a lot of Bill residing in each of us. It is the pressure and pace of business that brings out the Bill in you and me. Remember my example about the rumble bars and how they let us know we are getting off track? Learn from Bill how easily we can become adversarial in our dealings with others. When the pressure is on and the bottom line is sagging, it is easy for us to turn on the consumers and begin to work at conquering them.

Anne actually did see these people differently from Bill. Where Bill saw dollar signs, she saw the real need. Bill was right. They were wasting money on an inferior product, but he saw it as a deficiency in them, whereas Anne saw it as a genuine need. Instead of being cynical, she approached the situation with compassion. For a long time she had realized the limited choices the town's people had for quality goods. She couldn't do anything about all of the products, but she did have the ability to do something about their candles. She also realized that her customers did not recognize their need as keenly as she did. It wasn't that they were stupid or careless with their money. Anne knew it was just a matter of their being accustomed to doing things a certain way. Habits will trump many things, including good purchasing decisions. If the people knew what she and Bill had to offer, they would be buying every candle the two of them could make. But they didn't.

This observation falls under the heading of "people don't know what they don't know." You know you have a better product or service and offer a greater value, but the consumers don't know it. It is very difficult to reeducate people. Really, how well do you like it if someone tells you even in the nicest way that you are stupid? The only way you can begin to cause change in others is take the time to understand their present behavior. What drives their buying habits? In this case, the people have a supplier they know who supplies them regularly with a product that serves their basic need. Why should they go through all the disruption necessary to change that habit? At this point, it's not as important for the customers to know they could have a greater value as it is important for Anne to know that. As long as she knows, she can have a positive impact on others. If she identifies a *genuine* need and perseveres to meet it, she will be successful.

It is not enough for the need to be real for you, you have to be honest and see if it is really a need for your consumers.

Today, you can gather more statistical data about the marketplace in a few minutes than you can read and interpret in a week. We have data mining software that can tell us things we can't even understand. We need programs that translate the reams of data into a form our human minds can comprehend. Buried under this mountain of data and reports, we can no longer see the persons it was based on. We become like Bill and just see consumers' money directed our way. Anne sees more than that. She sees people who have value and opinions that matter. They are not just people with money to buy her candles, but people with homes, families, and lives that matter to them. They do not earn their value when they become customers, but bring intrinsic value to the marketplace every time they come. Instead of looking to the town's people to enhance her business, Anne was looking at her ability to enhance their lives further. Yes, further. Bill saw their lives as meaningless unless they were customers. Anne saw it as a value in and of itself whether or not they ever bought anything from her.

There is a huge gap between the advertisements that say you will be someone when you have our product and those that say you are somebody already and we would like to make your life better. One is condescending; the other respectful of who the consumer already is. You aren't going to win people over if you see yourself as the determiner of their value. *You win people over when you respect their value.*

Bill also saw the people as making a bad choice every time they bought the cheap candles off the wagon. Anne was willing to recognize that the people had a choice. You know, come to think of it, all people have a choice. Even if you are the only one with a product, people can choose to live without it. You may not like their choice, but you have to be able to respect that they have one.

Anne knew that, even though she had a better candle and a better value, the people did not *have* to buy from her. Come to think of it, people don't have to buy your product or service either. Do you respect that or resent it? Until you accept the consumers' right to have a choice, you are not going to do the work to get them to change their buying habits. Your goal is to be their new choice, but that is not going to happen until you accept that they are exercising their right to choose something else right now.

Let Go!

The final thing that Anne understood was that this was not an issue of selling something, but one of other people taking ownership. Remember how Bill wanted everyone to tell people that the candles were from Bill's Candle Shoppe? Well, what appeared to be good marketing was actually far from good. Anne understood that, when someone took her candles home and displayed them, she was not going to be the first one to get credit. When someone bought one of her candles, that customer was going to take it home and show it off.

Here is the difference Anne understood. Her customer would ask a visitor: "Would you like to see _my_ new candles?" The person would not ask if someone wanted to see the candles from Anne's Candle Shoppe. The customers were the beneficiaries of all Anne's hard work and years of experience. It was _their_ prize to show off and not Anne's.

This is really important to understand. You are letting people take ownership of something that you made, created, or did. They are going to see it as a reflection of their wisdom and personality, not yours.

"Look at *my* new car."

"Look at *my* new jeans."

"Look at *my* new book."

"Look at *my* new computer."

"Look at *my* new hairdo."

"Look at *my company's* new jet."

"Look at *our town's* new park."

Do you get it? You have to realize that you are transferring ownership of something to someone else. That person has every right to use it as an expression of himself. If you cannot share the ownership of your product or service and all the adoration and pride that goes with it, you are terminally egotistical. You have to grasp the fact that you are going to be partners in the ownership of your product with those you sell it to. Bill never was going to let go of his title to the candles. Anne knew from the beginning she would be giving it up.

When your customer is done gloating over everyone's adoration of his or her new purchase, what do you think the very next thing the admirers are going to ask? "Where did you get it?" Hello! Let go! Help the customers gloat and be proud, and they will let the secret out about your business. Just be sure you make them the proud and proper owners of what you have to offer. Respect their ownership. And next time I buy a car from you, don't put your dealership sticker on it. It's my car now and I will tell people where I got it if I want to.

Some of you have jumped to the conclusion that Anne was able to be more sensitive because she was a woman. I could retort that she is smarter because she is a woman. Now that all you women have highlighted that line, let's come back down to earth. The reality is that neither gender, race, age, nor anything else has anything to do with being smart. Making good decisions is what being smart is all about and not even a high IQ can trump that.

Anne is a smart and successful business person because she values other people. It's not a touchy-feely thing, it's all about having a respect for the value of all people, whether they buy from you or not. If you value them, I cannot guarantee they will change their habits and buy from you, but I can almost guarantee that if you don't respect them, they will never be your customers.

You decide if you are going to fight yourself or others. You decide if you will value others and seek to increase their value instead of your own. Do the former and you will have the latter. You can choose. Think of the difference your company could make if your employees actually valued each customer as a person.

Take Action

to show initiative

Hint: This chapter is closely tied to the next one, so you really need to read them at one sitting, if you can.

Years ago, someone told me that nothing has happened until you sell something. At the time, I was actually naive enough to believe them, and for years I followed that advice. Today, I think it is the dumbest thing I have ever heard. A lot should happen prior to a sale. I mean, it sounds like a great "Rah Rah" salesman thing to say, but it's more caveman like. Think stone tools compared to state-of-the-art lasers. First of all, everything is sales, because you are always attempting to sell something. Therefore, all business people are salespeople on one level or another.

The thing is, most people view the salesman as a gunslinger who is fast on the draw and can hit anything with pinpoint accuracy. The ideal salesperson is fast and accurate at closing the deal. I like to think of the salesperson as more of a cowpoke. He is out on the range rounding up all the dogies and eating dust day in and day out. But instead of getting them one at a time like the gunslinger, the cowpoke has a huge payday when he or she brings the herd to market. Yee haw! Sorry, too many metaphors, but you see what I am saying.

The goal always seems to be closing the deal for your idea in a meeting or closing a sale in the field with a client. That's the prize everyone is focused on. Yet, people are stumbling all over themselves because, instead of watching their steps, they are fixated on the sale. That's where you would expect to find Bill right now. He is obsessed with making all the sales he can, but he is doing a terrible job of it. Like so many, Bill doesn't understand how to get where he wants to go because he is too focused on getting there. It's like the first-time father who gets so excited when his wife goes into labor that he drives like a maniac to the hospital only to realize he ran off without his wife.

Bill is focused on one thing about himself —his ability to make a quality candle. All he ever thinks about is his candles and how much better they are than anyone else's and how to get people to buy them. Sell, sell, sell! How can he sell more candles and quickly corner the market and run Anne out of business?

He had one idea; that was to demonstrate how much better his candles were than the cheap ones. Bill put one of his candles right up in the front window and lit it. Right next to it, he put one of the cheap candles and lit it. The cheap candle quickly burned out, so he left its melted remains there and lit another cheap candle right next to it.   Every morning he would light his candle and the cheap one, and let them burn. He was going to visually prove to people how much more value they would get from his candles. After a few days, he had burned up eight of the cheap candles, but his candle still had some life in it. He would point out the display to all who came by and then ask how much money they were wasting on candles. In all, his candle lasted longer than eleven of the cheap ones, but his sales didn't increase. People were not that interested in Bill because he was not really interested in them.

Well, one person was interested in Bill; the traveling salesman, because Bill was becoming a pretty good customer for cheap candles.

Bill actually was a pretty talented man. He could do many other things and was well versed in many areas. Most of those things he pursued or studied when he was off work. When Bill was working, it was all about candles and selling them. He never considered all the other things he could do as useful because he never thought his customers needed anything but better candles—his! Bill saw his relationship with his customers as a one-step relationship: he made candles and they bought them (or were supposed to buy them). Closing more sales was all Bill ever focused on.

Courtship, Communication, and Results

This is where you can actually take off and do something in your business. Remember how this is a relationship and not a transaction? Think again about the young man wanting to have a date. How fast do you think he would scare off the girls if, on the first date, he started talking about marriage, kids, and a mortgage? Most women would find such talk offensive and presumptuous. They want to be courted first. They want time to be sure the young man is right for them. The same is true in the customer relationship. The length of the courtship and the depth of the relationship has to be in direct proportion to the expenditure. For a multi-million dollar contract, the courtship might last months or even years; but for a pack of gum, just greet me with a smile and say thank you when the transaction ends.

There is an ultimate goal to all business, but many steps. By the way, the ultimate goal is not a sale, but a mutually beneficial relationship.

Not all sales produce a relationship, but most relationships result in a sale. It's like dating. You don't get married on your first date. It's first date, second date, first kiss (I'm old-fashioned), more dates, first "I love you," more dates, first fight, timeout, makeup, more dating, meet the parents, more dating, proposal, planning, wedding, and then live happily ever after. Wow, that was a lot of work. Yes, but it was also a lot of steps. It was one elongated conversation that led to an agreement of some kind. You need to remember that this is not a book about sales, but about communication in the marketplace that will lead to relationships and then sales, donations, or contracts. *Don't confuse the two!*

Anne Does Something

Now along comes Anne. Okay, I know, she has now grown to the level of Miss Goody-Two-Shoes, but come on, I have to have a good and a bad example if we are ever going to get through this. Anne knows that sooner or later she has to make a sale, but she also knows some steps leading up to it are essential. She takes the initiative and starts moving people toward her. Too many companies try to lure people with fancy rhetoric, but people are getting wise to this. Anne could stand on the street corner every day and wax eloquently about her candles, but it wouldn't be effective. Remember her impact? Anne has to start moving people into a position where she can have an impact in their lives. She does this by understanding the little impacts that will move them the right way.

Anne has to list as many of her customers' needs as she can, regardless of whether she can meet them right now or not. She has to be careful that she does this from their perspective and not her own. You may think I need something, but I am only going to seal the deal based on what I think I need, even if I'm wrong. You get into dangerous territory when you try to sell someone on something he doesn't know he needs. If you can't define the need from the marketplace's perspective, you will either deliver inferior value or work yourself to death overselling. Why not try to hit the nail on the head?

Anne knows that people need to light their homes. Technically, the cheap candles are doing that to a level they have come to accept. Are Anne and Bill's candles better? Yes. The thing is, though, people don't know that yet.

Never presume how much credibility you have in the marketplace, because the minute you do, you will quit respecting the consumers' right to choose, and consequently you will start losing market share. Market credibility is hard to earn but easy to lose, so don't rely on it too much.

Anne is also realizing that being able to make a great candle and run a shop is not going to be enough. She is going to have to learn or utilize other skills in order to help the town's people become customers. The step of switching lifelong loyalties from the traveling salesperson is just too big for most people. She realizes these people will still have to see this person every month when they buy their other goods. They have a relationship with the traveling salesman that Anne is trying to invade. If Anne wants to sell candles to these people, she has to build the bridge for them to make the move.

You, the business owner, have to not only know where you want to get your customers, but also build the road or bridge to get there. It's something that happens in a progression of steps and responses. People need help in taking the big steps in life. It isn't sufficient simply to tell them to do so.

You must get into proximity with your customer in order to have a relationship. It works just as well to have them come to you as for you to go to them, depending on your type of business. In most cases, it will involve a little of both. So most businesses, like Bill's, will jump right out into the marketplace and get into the proximity of their customers. What they have failed to do is make the other people want to be around them. Getting into the proximity of someone who does not want to be in the proximity of you is called chasing that person. People know when you're doing it.

Most people would substitute advertising and marketing at this point. While you need advertising and lots of it, this is not what I am talking about. This is important for you to understand. Many companies have the majority of their conversations with the marketplace (remember, this is a book about communication) through advertising and marketing campaigns. That's sort of like having a long-distance romance via email and texting. You can only take the relationship to a certain level. Take Anne's business. She can hang signs all over town and at every crossroad for her Candle Shoppe, but that is not going to be enough to get people to buy her candles.

Beyond Advertising

Recently, a TV advertisement showed a little pig hanging out a car window. It held a pinwheel and squealed "weeeeeee" all the way home, much to the annoyance of everyone in the car. I think it is so funny, and I often do that very thing on the way home from a long day of shopping. Somehow, my wife does not share my admiration for the commercial and ducks down in the car so no one can see her. But here's the point, unlike the soda commercial with the inner tubes, for the life of me I can't tell you what company was featured in the piggy commercial. The commercial was entertaining, but a total waste of money to the company that wanted to pull me into their conversation.

We have way too much stupidity in the advertising conversation today. Cute is all right, but it doesn't persuade me to part with my hard earned money.

Since Anne did not use the piggy-ad agency, she knows she has to "do" something to engage the marketplace. She has to persuade consumers to make one step toward her, and that will involve some skills she can share other than those involved in candlestick making. She has the candlestick making skill down pat, but it's not the right tool to initiate the relationship. While her core competency will be very important later, right now she needs to do something else to get the ball rolling her way.

Her passion and impact are centered on people having elegant lighting in their homes no matter what their budget. One of the obstacles is that people don't realize their current lighting could be better. They use the same candles in the same place. It's a habit they have become accustomed to. Somehow, Anne has to help them see the possibilities in their own home. She thought about this and remembered all the fun she had setting up the home scenes in her store window. It did seem to be a point of conversation for people who stopped by, but they didn't make the connection with their own home or shop. What if she helped them make the connection by setting up candles in their homes?

Starting that day, when people commented on the window display, Anne asked if she could come by and offer some free lighting ideas for their home or office. At first, people didn't know what to make of her offer, but she assured them it was free. A few people started inviting Anne to look at their lighting.

She didn't enter the homes and tell the owners where they were wrong, even though she could have. Instead, she focused on their needs and asked them where they would like to have better lighting. One woman wanted more light in her parlor because she made extra money for the family by knitting scarves that the traveling salesman bought from her to sell. Another woman wanted light in the corner of a room where she did the accounting at night for her bakery. The bookkeeper in town said he had plenty of light over his desk, but Anne did not think so. What he wanted was more light over his bookshelves, because he was always putting one customer's ledger away and getting out a new one. He had trouble reading the names on the binding.

Anne would also take her candles along and, if a homeowner needed one, she would offer one of hers free. Homeowners almost always accepted the offer and she placed it in a prominent spot.

Do Something

This is not the first time we have heard of a free sample, but how do you usually get a free sample? Most often, it is dumped in your mailbox with little fanfare as a "we-hope-you-use-it-and-happen-to-like-it" attitude. Anne was actually engaged with the customer's needs.

I'll admit that I don't want you hand delivering free pantyhose to my wife and offering to help her put them on, but you know what I mean. The competition for customers today is fierce, and you not only have to be doing something value added to move them your way, but also you have to help them connect the dots.

Billions of dollars every year go into telling customers what you can do, but little or nothing goes into _showing_ them how to benefit from a product or service. People want to see what you can do. They are not going to jump the fence until they actually can see the greener grass growing and realize they can eat it. Today, companies are just telling us about the grass or showing us a silly piggy hanging out the window.

I don't expect Ford to send each of us a new car as a sampler, but there is something every company can do to reach out to the marketplace. It's a lot like shaking hands with someone. If you just extend your hand, they most likely will give you the benefit of the doubt and extend theirs. That's what you have to do. Initiate the handshake and quit standing around with a sign that was created by an ad agency and a graphics designer that says "We Want to Shake Your Hand." Just stick your hand out and let the consumers know you want to get to know them. Just think of the change in your organization if everyone started reaching out and building bridges for your customers.

Just the other day, as Anne was leaving a customer's home where she had helped with the placement of her candles, the peddler's wagon passed by. It was singing clip-clop and clink and clang as it slowly rolled along the road with all its wares swaying in an unrehearsed dance from their crowded positions on the wagon. The old peddler waved and smiled as he went about his rounds. Anne smiled and waved back, and then the light went on. She bolted from the porch and ran to catch up to the peddler, knowing he had to buy all his candles from someone, too. She's no dummy.

Cause a Response

to move forward

I am going to confuse you. I know that's a cardinal sin for a writer, but I have to do so in order to help you understand. Here I go. This step has to follow the preceding step, but in order to implement the preceding step correctly you must first know what is going to happen in this step. Think of these two steps as cause and effect. The previous step was cause; this one is effect. You need to know the effect you will create, and that step will determine the cause. In business, you have to have a target effect for every cause you perform. Know the very next thing your customer needs to do, and then create the perfect antecedent.

In the past, we taught people a "proven" set of causes based on years of experience. Today, we have so many new technologies, products, and markets, that there are no proven methods to penetrate them. Now you have to know what unique effect you need and how to create the cause yourself.

Market interaction is not a one-step process. Most owners and companies see the delivery of their goods or services as the primary outcome. It really isn't. Yes, you have to deliver goods and services at a profit to stay in business, but you also have to know all the steps in the process as well as what you're really trying to accomplish. Failure to see a bigger picture is the reason most companies have to keep reinventing themselves and continually acquire new customers.

If you remember, this is a conversation aimed at creating, maturing, and continuing relationships. The response you are looking for has to be just the right size. If the response is too big a step, it will scare people off. If the step is too small, they won't realize you're taking them somewhere. It has to be just the right size for your audience.

This is where the winners and the losers in the markets start at the same place and arrive at two very different destinations. Bill and Anne both know the people of their town need to change their candle-buying habits. The current way of purchasing candles is to buy a very low-quality product at an inflated price. Bill and Anne agree on this. The difference comes in how and

The Candlestick Wars

what to communicate. If you can't provide a superior product, price, or value, you have lost before you've even begun. Bill does offer all three elements of improvements to his customers, but he can't seal the deal.

Perceptions

Bill's focus is on reiterating the problem to the potential customers. He knows they will never have good lighting in their homes as long as they buy the cheap peddler candles. He has tried and tried to convince people of the error of their purchasing ways. But how many of us like to be told we are doing something wrong? Usually, telling someone they should not be doing something just makes that person more determined to do it. While it's true people could use a better-quality product, telling them they're purchasing the wrong thing is not going to make them change their buying habits.

If we're going to believe in the product we offer, we had better know that it is better than the competition's. A very bright and talented former student of mine quit a job because she didn't believe in the product. She knew her efforts to promote it would fall flat if she didn't think it was a quality product. You are no different. You have to believe you're offering a greater value to people. Armed with this confidence, too many companies and sales people are trying to win markets with

60

the attitude of: "Hey, I'm convinced this is a great product, and you're making a mistake if you don't buy it."

Some companies spend millions of dollars trying to convince consumers that their product is better than the competition's. Quality and value are important, but not at this point in the conversation. You have to believe it, but it is counterproductive to think others will immediately see it and buy your product. To the consumers, this sounds like: "Trust me! Would I lie to you?"

Bill is trying to make and sell candles based on the fact that "he" believes it is a better deal. It is a better deal, but not in his customers' minds, at least, not yet! That's the important part to understand. The value people use in *all* purchasing decisions is a *perceived* value. The perception is theirs, not yours! I repeat, the perception is theirs and *not yours*. So, the issue becomes one of changing their perceptions to the point where their perceived value matches the price you are asking. This is true even if you're running a volunteer non-profit. The personal impact people make from volunteering must match a perceived value in their thinking. They must see the price of time they are paying gives them an equal or greater sense of fulfillment through service.

Actions and Emotions

This isn't an intellectual exercise. You can't argue, discuss, or regurgitate enough facts for someone to make a purchase. No matter how much research people do, the final decision is based on emotions. Yes, we make emotional decisions. The downside to this is that many people exploit this fact by resorting to manipulation. Bill's few customers buy from him because he guilts them into buying. He is not making customers; he is making enemies. His customers will take his candles home, see the difference, and like them. But then they will go to Anne's shop for future purchases. In their mind, Bill is a jerk, and they don't want him to have the satisfaction of being right.

We usually get things backwards in business because we want a shortcut. We all know "haste makes waste." The general rule of thumb is to make an emotional appeal of some sort so people will act. I mean, after all, it seems like I have been urging that. No, I haven't. Most people are under the impression that actions follow feelings. When actions follow emotions, it is a knee-jerk reaction that the consumer soon identifies as buyer's remorse. How would you like your customer to tell their friends they bought your product but probably shouldn't have?

In reality, relationships and decisions work just the opposite. Take the impulse items at the checkout of your local store. You get in the shortest line to save your precious time. As you stand there, you "look" at the candy rack next to you, and begin to "explore" the items there. All of a sudden, you "see" one of your favorite candy bars, and wow, all of a sudden you "feel" like having a candy bar.

The store owner knows you will look at those racks out of boredom while standing in line and that action will lead to a feeling of hunger or need of something displayed there. What if you could utilize that process in all your business dealings and understand what the ultimate goals are?

Anne understood this and actually did it. Remember, she went to people's homes and helped them rearrange their lighting. She was not trying to get them to buy candles, as you might suppose. People already had candles and this is what Bill couldn't grasp. He and Anne are not in the candle business. *If you don't understand your impact, then you will lead people and yourself to a dead end every time!*

Follow how simple this is. If people realized they wanted better lighting in their homes, they would recognize the candles they are now using aren't good enough. Second, if they have a desire for better candles, what are they going to do? They are going to find a new supplier—probably

Anne because she has built a relationship with them.

Open Their Eyes First

If people recognize their need, you will be able to meet the need. The goal you should be working toward is of helping them see a greater need that your product or service will fulfill. Anne employed a two-step approach to accomplish this. Her goal was not to force, manipulate, or coerce consumers into a decision. Her goal was to take them through a process in which the decision would be theirs. When the purchasing decision belongs to the customer, he or she will brag about their purpose every time! And do you remember the first question people will ask? That's right: "Where did you get it?"

Anne went into the homes of consumers and let them determine the scope of their need. Her goal was not to sell them candles but to show them how to have better lighting throughout their homes. The best place for her to start was their point of greatest perceived need.

Don't underestimate the importance of perception. If you can help a person in his greatest area of perceived need, he will naturally make the connection you can help him in all other areas.

The issue you first need to address with consumers is that of bringing a solution to their problem within the realm of possibility. Anne's customers had given up on an improved way of lighting their homes. Years of endless attempts to use cheap candles to light their homes better had left them at the edge of their known technology. In other words, this was as good as they thought it could get because they didn't really understand that there was a difference in candles' quality. Anne had to demonstrate (an action) that things could be better. She had to help them discover the possibilities so they would have a reason to respond. You have to show, and not just make a claim.

As Anne showed consumers the change in lighting, they needed to perceive that change as positive. When people responded to Bill, it was a negative response to get him off their backs. There was nothing positive about it. When Anne was done, people would say: "Hey, I (not Anne) improved the lighting in my home." What do people say when they respond to you or your company? Is it positive or negative? Don't be seen as a necessary evil (Bill), but as a solution provider (Anne).

Anne knew she wanted people to respond by _seeing_ how they could improve the lighting in their home. Bill wanted people to _buy_ a candle or two from him. Anne wanted them to _see_ a possibility because she understood it was the next and doable step in the relationship she was building with prospective customers. She was not trying to persuade people to buy candles, but to improve the lighting in their home.

Anne knew that as soon as consumers corrected the problem in their greatest area of perceived need they would change every other area of need in their home. She has not only moved them to the place of change, but has also initiated the next process of change. I told you she was no dummy!

Necessary Steps

The number of steps and the amount of time it takes to get through the steps will vary depending on the size of the transactions. If you begin to understand the next two things I share, that understanding will change the way you approach any market with any product.

First, you have to understand and use the process of action and reaction. You cannot sit in the marketplace broadcasting tons of rhetoric to consumers. Every day people are overwhelmed with words and images. Not that you discard these, but realize you have to "do" something besides just talk. Understand the power of extending your hand for a handshake or just smiling at people. You have to actually do something that makes people respond. Nike® makes people think about the possibility of being a winner by showing how great athletes win with

Nike® gear. Even if their sport gear has only a placebo effect, it still causes people to react with a perception of being on the winning team. Their goal is to make people think about their own abilities using Nike.

Second, you have to understand that the movement to closing any deal is a process of steps. Instead of just looking at the prize and tripping all the way there, start thinking about the necessary steps for you and your customers. Start in the area of their greatest perceived need and work out from there. *Don't force them to consider your greatest strength, but solve their greatest need.* Then, take things one step at a time to help them arrive where they feel as though they are the owners of a good decision to buy or use your product or service. These steps are a conversation.

Everyone cheers the "Hail Mary" pass in the final seconds of the game, but it's a long shot. A football coach told me that the goal of the game was to move the ball three or four yards every time it was snapped. Being able to march the ball down the field in a consistent increment every play is what makes a team great. He must have known, because he ultimately won a state championship.

Hardly anything in this world moves in giant leaps without a catastrophic input. Think earthquakes and hurricanes. Life, people, relationships, conversations, businesses, politics, and markets all move in incremental steps, not leaps. Think carving the Grand Canyon.

If you can master the art of incremental movement of people, products, services, and ideas, you can conquer markets.

What could happen in your business if your employees became masters of the incremental process of helping customers become empowered to make their own decisions, which moves them to a point where they have to have your service or product? It boggles the mind, doesn't it?

Deliver Quality

to create loyalty

There is nothing worse than trying to push a rock up a hill only to have it roll back down before you get to the top. That's exactly how most people push their businesses and careers. You can't stop doing the hard work of rolling that rock until you crest the hill. This is the goal you have to accomplish. Those who persevere to the top have the best chance of making it in the marketplace.

The first real battle you had to win was the one against yourself; getting to the top is the second battle you must win. At this point many things come into play. It has likely frustrated you that I haven't given much credit to quality, price, and delivery. If you work very hard at these things, you can stand up now and take a bow.

Look at what you've done so far. First, you defined the impact you wanted to make in the world. Second, you realized how your passion could be shared with others. With that foundation, you started building a relationship with a specific group of people. You created an action that would bring a predetermined response; one that was both positive and doable. But, you haven't won the consumers yet.

Almost There

After people respond to your action, there is a slight pause while they assess the outcome of this interaction. They're waiting to see if the outcome of their response is going to meet their expectations. They want to see if they have made a good or bad decision.

You can't answer this question for them directly. You can only help answer this question based on the statement your product or service makes. This is the part that Bill was so confident about. He had great skills and made a great product, but that wasn't enough to gain a customer. He wasn't willing to do the work needed to get people to this point. He just wanted to skip all the other steps. Relationships were sterile and of little importance to him.

Small businesses and people in the science and engineering fields seem to struggle with this the most. The irony is, if you can't get them to this point, all the quality in the world won't matter, because you'll be broke.

I want you to imagine watching Bill nail up the windows of his Candle Shoppe and taking down his sign. He could have succeeded if he had built relationships and carried on a conversation in his marketplace. However, he was totally consumed with telling people they would be happy once they tried his product. This tragedy is repeated in businesses today. Everyone in your organization must know the importance of having a conversation to build relationships. Even many mid- and upper-level executives don't know some of these things, and this fact drives the CEO crazy.

These people aren't _bad_ business people. They just need to be better at communicating and building relationships. Bill was a great candlestick maker, but his business folded because of what he didn't know or wouldn't do. He had all the technical skills he needed, but he lacked conversational skills. He couldn't get beyond products and processes to actually connect with his customers. He wanted to promote his products instead of building bridges to get the products into the customers' hands where the products would speak for themselves. Wave goodbye to Bill, because he never got far enough for people to find out how good his candles were.

"But," you may protest, "our customers want to know about us and our product." The ticket price of what you are offering will determine how much you are vetted prior to this point. The recommendations you get will be only a reflection of the previous relationships you had, not just the work you did. But, know for certain that after the sale, each customer is going to decide for himself or herself if your product was a quality investment or not. He is not going to become a lifelong customer based on your references. His customer loyalty will be defined by his or her interaction with you and nothing else.

Bigger and Better

In your strategic plan, this is where you analyze yourself with a critical and honest eye. Never put yourself in a position where you are just asking your customers to make a horizontal shift. You have to know you are a step up in quality, service, knowledge, price, opportunity, or whatever else it is you offer as a competitive advantage.

Once people make the decision to leave their old supplier, they had better be happy right away. They must see an immediate, tangible difference from their response to you. Change is difficult, even if it involves changing only the brand of milk we buy. If your customers do not see a significant difference from their old way of doing things, they will revert back to where they bought before you became their supplier. You have earned only the right to be *tested* up to this point.

Your Big Audition

You must understand what's happening right now. Most people, including Bill, think they are home free once the deal is closed. Actually, you have just now entered center stage for your audition. I am still auditioning for you in this book because you have not finished *testing* the product for yourself. The same is true when you make a sale.

Many companies relax at this point because they have the false impression that they have the customer in the bag. Not so. At this point, you are in the position of being a change agent for your customers. They are entertaining the idea of making you their new normal. Even if this is a one-time multi-million dollar contact, you're attempting to be the firm the customer recommends to others. Because you will become a new part of their story and their history, you need to make good on it.

Your customer is in a transformational state right now. It's a time of flux for their habits and perceptions. If you quit now, the rock will roll back down the hill and you will have done all this work for nothing.

Anne's customers are assessing if her candles really are a better value. They are critiquing the improvement in their lighting. They are deciding if they can connect with Anne as they did with the traveling peddler. Everything is new to them and up for debate. Discussion will take place in each home about whether they like the change or not. Anne will be personally assessed and discussed. So, after the sale, the real scrutiny begins.

Anne will have to treat the new relationship very carefully. Things are fragile and could go either way. She will have to follow up and make sure the outcomes have met each customer's expectations. She has to be extremely flexible and adaptable.

After any sale, tensions are high. You are under the microscope. The higher the cost, the more intense the scrutiny. If I buy something as minor as a new brand of gum, I will pause when I put that first piece in my mouth and focus on whether I like the taste or not. At this point, most companies go into their "work" mode. Their thinking is that they have the job, or the sale, so let's transition over to doing what we do best. You really have to perform at this point, but it is not simply another performance, it is opening night, and all the critics are in the front row.

Many companies don't get repeat business, or strain the working relationship, because they quit courting their customer as soon as the sale is closed. It's like the young man who bought his girlfriend flowers and candy all the time they were dating, but once they married he couldn't even remember his wife's birthday. Your company can't be like that. This is *the* time to put your best foot forward, whether the consumer is a first-time customer or a longtime one.

How do you think customer service would change in your company if the people on the front lines understood this? What would happen to quality if people realized they were auditioning instead of just performing their appointed tasks? What if an engineer, a waitress, a CPA, a doctor, a truck driver, or a lawyer saw their role this way? What if they were aware of their part in the relationship with the marketplace while they were doing their job? You would have a company full of customer-change agents.

Earning Trust

You are now in the phase where you have to earn people's trust. Remember how Kennedy, Reagan, and Obama won their elections based on projecting an impact and a shared passion with people? There came a point in their administrations when they had to have outcomes to match those factors. People did not *give* them their vote, they *loaned* it to them based on a promise of expected outcome.

This is what sank the effectiveness of George W. Bush's second term. He took the election as a "mandate" and "political capital" and all the people said was that they liked the first dance and were willing to have a second. President Bush took it as "I got the girl now so I'll drag her home," and he left the dance floor.

Every time we sell a service or product, it has to match our promises. This is the first thing people look at. Our promise is the impact we have been identified with. In other words, customers are looking to see if we are who we say we are. But, here is the tough part. *It will be based on their perception of the outcome we deliver and not on our own perception.* The more shallow the impact, the easier it will be for them to depart.

Bill's impact was to sell a candle with better value. Anne's impact was to give better light in each person's home or business. Bill's impact had only a monetary value. Anne's had a richer life value. The further you can project your impact into the consumer's life, the further you can extend the outcome and the more likely you are to transform them. This approach also gives you a broader platform to be judged on. It gives you more time to prove your trustworthiness, which is what people want. Consequently, for people to change their buying habits, your trustworthiness has to convince them you have and can keep delivering.

A carmaker cannot make just one good model; all its models have to be of the same quality. A store cannot have just a few good sales people; they all have to be good. *People need to see trustworthiness in your company's outcome no matter what is delivered or who delivers it.* That is how long-term trust is built, so don't leave human or product gaps in your company!

Give Hope

Finally, the outcome has to give them hope. Anne helped people transform one area or one room of their home with new candles. The outcome had to be such that customers could readily see the application of her candles in other areas. They had to be hopeful that this was the beginning of something that would benefit them in additional areas and/or over a long period of time.

If I go to a new doctor and she is able to help me with one ailment, I will naturally assume she can help me with future ailments. At this point, she doesn't have to make that connection for me; I'll do it myself. I will always hold the doctor under a degree of scrutiny, but less so now because I am going to give her the benefit of the doubt. Every time you audition for someone and win the part, they will feel more comfortable with you.

This is that magic watershed we are all reaching for called "customer loyalty." *Never assume you have it, and never take it for granted.*

Teach everyone in your organization that every day, every sale, and every job is an audition with your customers. Teach them that they must never relax but always see themselves as change agents for their customers. Help them understand that even the most technical skills need to be wrapped in the powerful package of a strong and growing conversation with every customer.

Make your company's culture one that sees everyone from the top floor to the basement as personally responsible for, and empowered to, make a difference in the business' relationship with the marketplace. How would *that* change your bottom line?

See the Future

to be the leader

Time has moved on for Anne and her business. She's had a good relationship with her town and made a good living for many years. She's been hearing talk of a new way to light the world. Something called a "lamp" is being used in the big cities. It uses oil for fuel and candlestick makers all across the country are starting to lose business. Anne has always been a great candlestick maker, but her true passion has always been light, no matter how it is made. Anne wrote a letter to a lamp maker to see if she could learn more.

Many businesses and business people think and plan for tomorrow, but few actually do anything about it until tomorrow arrives. Failure to act isn't always a matter of procrastination or apathy, but of skills. Industry foresight is one thing; becoming the vehicle that gets everyone there is another. That's where industry leaders leave the pack of competitors behind. Being ready for the future is what those in second place do. Being the first to arrive in the future with a strong customer base is what the leaders do. Which do you want to be?

It doesn't take a genius to see the inevitability of the future, but it does take a very wise business to predict the changes that will define the future. Those who never see the impending changes are the customers. Their propensity is to live in the present and not change until they are forced to. Think HDTV.

In order for your company or organization to have a future, you have to be in the business of connecting the dots between the past, the present, and the future – for yourself and your customers. You have to know exactly what is going to happen and how to shape the conversation. People in the marketplace don't want to be told about the future; they want you to talk them through it. They don't want a fortuneteller; they want a guide.

The minute your company or organization begins to see itself as a safe port in the marketplace, you are dead. Your company is a ship; time is the port. You are here only for a moment, so you need to be moving from the present to the future. Companies that see themselves as the port always have to pack up and move to a new port (time). You have to be mobile. Your cry to the consumer is not, "Buy here," but rather, "All aboard!"

Don't put down roots in the port, but create a great ship with an awesome crew and navigation system. Always remember that people naturally love the port and don't think they will ever have to leave. They are not drawn to the high seas of change but to the *terra firma* of familiarity. You know if they stay here, it will eventually dry up and nothing will be left for them. You know it is urgent for them to get on a ship to the future, so it might as well be yours. You also know that people will resist coming on board no matter how much you warn them of impending doom if they stay.

Only two things will persuade people to get on your ship. The first is if you are the last one leaving port and they have no other choice. But that also means you will be the last ship to the future with less time to succeed. The other reason people will get onboard with you is because they trust you because you have always had an honest conversation with them.

Your ship will soon be leaving port, never to return again. You are taking your passengers somewhere they have not seen or heard about yet. They will always judge you by the last trip they took with you. Make every trip unforgettable so they will be ready to go with you the next time!

Let people see your crew busy and working to get the ship ready for sea. Don't tell them time is short, because they will grow indifferent to your nagging. Just keep their curiosity up. Don't let your crew waste the days away in port (the present), but see to it that they know the urgency of keeping the ship in tip-top shape and ready to sail at a moment's notice.

People will be able to tell the difference between your ship, where the crew is constantly working to get her ready, and the ships with no crew or those having crews that are sleeping on the deck. You will tell a story of the future ports of call by all the excitement you demonstrate in your activity. Your commitment of resources, manpower, and vision will say everything people need to hear. Your demonstration of urgency for the future will be infectious.

The future is a scary place for people. They need someone to do the work of providing a way to get there. They don't know what kind of computer, phone, medicine, car, or even toothbrush they will need in ten years. If they had to figure all these things out, nothing would change. But you know there will be innovations and competitors emerging who will try to steal your share of the market. If they succeed, your ship will sink.

People need options and flexibility for the long trip ahead. They need to know that the future is a journey requiring a tour guide, not an event requiring a ticket agent. Don't allow your employees to see themselves as those who punch customers' tickets. You are taking people into tomorrow, and you need to arrange for their safe and sound arrival.

Be the first to know that safe arrival is doable. Your people need to see it. They need to realize the possibility of taking a lot of people with them. As your crew works on your ship temporally at dock, people will walk by and engage crew members in conversation. Your frontline people should always be able to tell others where they are going and what the future looks like.

Too many companies fail to teach the vast majority of their employees (those not in sales) about critical business functions such as customer relations, acquisitions, retention, and the future. Even if they never speak to a customer, they need to know that what they do impacts the employees who *are* talking to customers. Like those who work in the engine room of the ship where they can't even see the ocean, they need to support those at the helm. The job of taking your customer base into the future is too great a task for just a few people to accept.

Create a sustainable future people can believe in. You absorb the waves of change so that their lives are not in upheaval. You must create the environment where they can transition in safety and confidence. They have to have the confidence that you can and will make the crossing safely. No matter how constant change is in this world, people want to know that there is a new normal on the horizon. They cannot comprehend the transcendence of normalcy nor its brevity. That is why they need you, your company, and your employees to build a long-term relationship with them in a conversation of trust. They will soon learn that you know where you are going and you can get them there safely. In all that you do, communicate to them a relationship that takes you both into tomorrow and beyond.

So now I have to ask. Did you forget what I told you not to do? Remember, I told you this was a book about communication. We seem to want to turn the all-important conversation with the marketplace into some sort of science, but it is nothing more than the ability to initiate, maintain, and project a dialogue based on both verbal and nonverbal communication. It involves the art of living a conversation in the marketplace. This is how you win in business. Will you win your own personal and corporate candlestick war? It's up to you.

I have been asking you all along how this would change your business. What would happen to the bottom line and the marketplace if you could teach this to everyone in your company? It is not so much a matter of your knowing this, but a matter of helping others know it and then having everyone do something about it.

How would the conversations in your boardrooms, team meetings, department meetings, and in the offices of your company change if people were thinking about these things? Aren't these the kind of things you want people talking and thinking about in your company? It has been such a simple story, but it's so true. Do you want your people to think like Bill or like Anne?

People who need this knowledge are your friends, your coworkers, your team, your boss, your employees, and, perhaps, even your family. The conversation starts only when others join in it. Give each of them a copy of this book, and begin to see what you can change together in your boardroom, office, business, corporation, and your world. This book creates just a little spark, but from that you can start a fire. Start your conversation, and see what results. Call me if you need help. I'll help you fan the flames so you can light your world.

Greatness is 7 steps away !

Make a difference ...
        to be known.

Share passion ...
        to be attractive.

Value others ...
        to show sincerity.

Take action ...
        to show initiative.

Cause a response ...
        to move forward.

Deliver Quality ...
        to create loyalty.

See the future ...
        to be the leader!

Share This Story

Now that you know these seven powerful, yet simple steps, think of what could happen if you share it with others! You can order individual copies of the book from Amazon.com. Also, it's available in digital form from Apple and Amazon.

If you would like to receive **quantity discounts** by ordering 25 or more books, please go to our website at:

www.communicateforward.com

Click on the book link. Imagine what would happen if everyone in your company understood the importance of these seven steps! For less than you would pay an average consultant, you can empower your whole organization!

More About the Author

The Candlestick Wars is based on Tim Buchanan's executive workshop titled "7 Steps to Greatness". Tim is a Strategic Dialogue Analyst and Teacher using a process called Full Spectrum Dialogues™. His goal is to help you create productive business conversations utilizing all your verbal and non-verbal resources. It's essential for internal customers, external customers, leaders, and success.

Full Spectrum Dialogues™ make the most out of every opportunity you have by fusing your strategy, message and customer relationships into one synergistic approach. We analyze where you can improve these interactions and provide strategic solutions. We enable you to create and sustain dialogues that produce long-term results.

If you would like your leaders to explore these dynamic principles in depth, please contact us to learn more. For more information, contact Tim Buchanan at either:

Email - tim@communicateforward.com
Phone - 303.517.0129

Or visit our website at:
www.communicateforward.com

The Candlestick Wars

The Candlestick Wars

The Candlestick Wars

The Candlestick Wars

The Candlestick Wars

The Candlestick Wars

[1] Walmart is registered trademark of Walmart, Inc.

[2] Nike is a registered trademark of Nike, Inc.

[3] Microsoft is a registered trademark of Microsoft Corporation in the United States and/or other countries.

[4] Apple is a registered trademark of Apple, Inc.

[5] Ford is a registered trademark of the Ford Motor Company.

[6] Quality is Job 1 is a registered trademark of the Ford Motor Company